HOW TO GET FINANCIALLY FREE IN 7 DAYS THROUGH PROPERTY

A Step-by-Step Instructional Guide

LEGAL NOTICES

TABLE OF CONTENTS

HOW TO GET FINANCIALLY FREE IN 7 DAYS THROUGH PROPERTY

"I did it and you can too." - Samuel Leeds

ABOUT THE AUTHOR

Samuel Leeds is a hugely successful property investor and the founder of one of the biggest training companies in the UK.

Samuel left school at 16 and, despite having no money, bought his first buy-to-let at a below market price just before his 18th birthday. He was too young to apply for a mortgage but got permission to put the house in a relative's name. After refinancing the property up to its true value, he paid off the bridging loan, pocketing a monthly profit of £950 in rent.

That modest home in Bournville, Birmingham, ignited a multi-million pound business. By the time Samuel was 19, his passive income from rents dwarfed the average person's salary. He realised early in life that property investing can lead to financial freedom and could have retired at 21.

The past 12 months have seen him investing in 30 properties and buying a 'castle' – historic Ribbesford House in Worcestershire. It was the place where General de Gaulle's Free French soldiers trained during WW2. The plan is to restore the imposing Grade II listed building to its former glory with a tasteful development of luxury apartments and holiday lets.

Samuel's investment strategies rely solely on knowledge and formulas, not feelings or luck.

Every single property in his portfolio, from his first buy-to-let to his grand country estate, was the result of a methodical approach.

He maintains, however, that the best investment he ever made was 'in myself.' Even as a 17-year old he had an unquenchable thirst for knowledge. Wearing an ill-fitting £30 suit from Asda, he attended specialist property events, constantly mixing with successful people.

Now aged 27, Samuel heads up a group of companies in the Midlands, which also includes a building company and lettings agency. The flagship of the group is Property Investors UK, which offers free, two-day crash courses across the country. Demand for the specialist training is great, with up to 1,000 people attending a single event. The courses, which attract rave reviews, are not just for people new to property investing who want to become financially free. They also attract experienced investors looking to improve their profits.

Many students on the Property Investors Crash Course opt for further advanced training and become members of the prestigious Property Investors Academy. In addition to receiving expert, one-to-one guidance on potential deals, they network with skilled investors, gaining priceless contacts in all areas of the property world.

Samuel's meteoric rise as a young entrepreneur has seen him appear on TV several times, as well as making headlines in the regional and national press.

He also attracts a large online audience through his YouTube channel and other social media.

In the summer of 2018, he was seriously injured while in Uganda checking on the progress of a charity project funded by his company to bring fresh water to a remote village – where many of the children had been suffering from bloated stomachs as a result of drinking water from a lake. Soon after arriving in the country, he shattered his kneecap after being thrown down a waterfall while white-water rafting. Following an emergency operation, he was flown back to England a fortnight later and told by doctors he would never walk properly again.

With his leg still in plaster, Samuel made headlines again when, in defiance of this prediction, he walked unaided up The Wrekin in Shropshire. Weeks later he decided to discard his wheelchair and donate it to a soldiers' charity.

The Financial Freedom Challenge took place four months after the accident and he completed it without the use of walking aids.

As a committed Christian, Samuel believes that the pursuit of wealth is a force for good as it provides the means to help others. The businessman donates ten per cent of his income to the Church and vital charities in Africa. In addition, he contributes to many other good causes in the UK. He has plans over the next year to further his work for the homeless, as well as provide a shelter for abused women and their children.

This is Samuel Leeds' third book. He is also the author of the best-selling Buy Low Rent High and Do the Possible, Watch God Do the Impossible.

Samuel lives in Lichfield, Staffordshire with his wife Amanda and two children.

FINANCIAL FREEDOM – IN A WEEK!

Without a penny to invest, young multi-millionaire property investor Samuel Leeds set off on an extraordinary undercover mission to prove he could become financially free again from scratch.
Samuel left home in an old banger and headed for a hotel which had been pre-booked for him in an unfamiliar city. He had to make money by the end of the week or face eviction.

Wearing a black wig and fake glasses, Samuel took on the alias of Lucas Ruby. He was denied access to his funds and could only deal with strangers. It was no stroll in the park and he was thrown out of a networking event when his cover was blown.
But within seven days of arriving in Sheffield the 27-year-old entrepreneur had made an incredible £8,000 from selling property deals. He immediately invested the money in two city centre apartments generating a monthly rental profit of approximately £2,000. On his return to Staffordshire, he stopped off at a homeless charity in Manchester to donate a £2,000 surplus from the challenge.

By adopting the same strategies he preaches to thousands of students each year, the property tycoon proved beyond doubt that knowledge is key to becoming financially independent. A YouTube video on the Financial Freedom Challenge attracted half a million views in a fortnight.
In this concise book Samuel Leeds explains in clear steps how he gained financial freedom in a week – and how YOU can too!

15

FOREWORD

I was a negative, sceptical Scotsman when I first saw Samuel on a BBC show about landlords which intrigued me, to say the least. In September 2017, I found myself standing with the other delegates waiting patiently for the doors to open at the Crash Course to find out if this guy was as good as all the rave reviews. I'm nervous and before I know it my inner doubts kick in. What am I doing here? There's no way this is going to work for me! Thankfully, I decided to make the most of the few days and see what happened.

Samuel struck me as a very positive and direct person. No small talk, no messing, just straight down to business. I really liked this as I'm very similar, so instantly warmed to him. Over the two days of the course he was very approachable and only too happy to help. My negativity and doubts were still whirling around my head, but thankfully Samuel has a way of installing a can-do attitude and building self-belief in people. I decided to put my trust in Samuel and myself, so resolved to do further training with him. That was the decision that has changed my life forever. In less than a year I have acquired my own property portfolio and run a successful deal sourcing business, while both my wife and I have quit our jobs.

I am often asked what Samuel is like to work with. All I will say on this is that when you make a move, he makes ten. Samuel has a very driven and no messing attitude. He expects his students to adopt the same attitude. This is something I really admire and I think is key to the success of his students. Too many people fail at their first rejection, whereas Samuel is like 'brush yourself off and pick up the phone!!' I've witnessed many sides of Samuel. He's a warrior when he needs to be and a genuinely caring person when required. The accident in Africa was a fine example of this. Even though he had shattered his kneecap and was in incredible pain, his thoughts were with the rest of the team and how they were feeling. He genuinely cares about his friends and students, and makes it his mission to ensure they are succeeding. I've witnessed him go above and beyond the call of duty to help people.

When Samuel told me about this crazy idea to start all over again with an alias name and no money, assets or credit, I was very impressed, albeit I thought he was mad! What other trainer in the world has made himself and his methods so vulnerable? I can't think of one. The risks were plain to see. What would happen if he failed? He risked people discrediting his techniques and teachings. To my surprise Samuel responded with no matter what happens, lessons will be learnt. He was more than happy to put himself out there for the benefit of his followers and students. He was so determined to prove that anyone with the right knowledge does not need lots of money to succeed in property. The results were amazing, and honestly I never doubted he would succeed.

There is no question that meeting Samuel has completely changed my life. I have found a very good friend and business partner, and was honoured to be asked to write this foreword. I wanted to take this opportunity to say thank you. I hope you know how much of an impact you have had on my life. You have made me believe in myself again which has made me a much more confident and driven person. My family's future is now so bright and you played a huge part in that.

Alasdair Cunningham, Author of "Whatever It Takes"

The Financial Freedom Challenge #FFChallenge

The title "Get Financially Free in 7 Days" is an outrageous statement, but I say this because I achieved it. In seven days I made £8,000 and acquired two high, cash-flowing rent-to-rent apartments. You will discover the step-by-step instructions that will enable you to do the same.

The reason I managed to do this so quickly is because I have done it before. When I was 17, I bought my first property. Nobody gave me a penny. I am from a working/middle class family and by the time I was 21 I was financially free. It meant my passive income was enough for me to live a comfortable life forever. Four years later, I was a property millionaire and am now a multi-millionaire. I own a 'castle', Ribbesford House in Worcestershire, and run one of the most successful training companies in the UK.

Making money is simply the result of having the correct knowledge and implementing it. When poor people win the lottery, they become poor again over time. If a rich person were to lose everything, they would become rich again over time. Therefore, rather than hoping to become wealthy one day, it is better to learn the skills to achieve that and simply make it happen. After a decade of owning property and being successful, I deeply desired to start all over again from scratch to prove to myself, and to the world, that with the right knowledge absolutely anybody can become financially free. Financially free means you are liberated from having to work in a regular job. In this instance my goal was to achieve a gross income of £3,000 per month. At least half of that had to be passive income, that is to say recurring money from rents that would continue coming in, even if I was sleeping.

On my Facebook group I posted the idea of starting all over again and called it the Financial Freedom Challenge (#FFChallenge). I got over 10,000 people asking me to do this.

Objective of the Challenge:

To build a property income of £3,000 per month from scratch. At least 50 per cent of this needs to be a passive/residual income. If I run out of money and cannot afford to live, or abandon the challenge without my income, I fail.

If I can prove to be financially independent any time after starting with nothing and then demonstrate I can make £3,000 a month through property, I succeed.

Purpose:

To prove that anybody can do this with the right knowledge and become financially free, regardless of their circumstances – no excuses.

Rules:

1. Money. I cannot invest a penny of my own money, nor do I have access to my bank account for anything.

2. Staff. I cannot get any of my staff to help or assist with this challenge in any way.

3. Network. I cannot take a penny from anyone in my existing network. Any properties I buy, or sell, have to be from strangers. Due to my name being quite well known in the property world, I will be using an alias.

4. I am allowed to travel as much as I like, but I will have to be based in a place where I do not know anybody and have no properties. This location will be pulled out of a hat on Facebook Live.

5. I will be evicted from my hotel on November 22, 2018, unless I have made enough money to pay for more nights.

6. I will begin the challenge with a new bank account – a compliant property company account with a balance of £0 and a zero credit rating. I will also be supplied with one week's worth of clothes, basic essentials and one week booked in a hotel room in the location.

7. I will have a referee with me at all times to make sure I stick religiously to the rules and will document the journey for my YouTube channel. If I succeed, I will have to go over all the profits and figures with a third party, independent professional who has experience in finance and property. He will assess and decide if my success is satisfactory, in line with the original goal.

7 Step Formula to Financial Freedom in 7 Days

Not only did I achieve this goal, but I did it in just seven days. All I did was follow seven simple steps that I will be sharing in each chapter of this book. Could anybody do it in a week? No, because newbies would need to allow time to learn the ropes first. Success is like driving a car. Once you have passed your driving test and been driving for years, it is second nature and extremely easy. However, it is always difficult at first and you always need an instructor. I hope to be a good instructor to you in this book. When you become successful, please do track me down to tell me because your success is my oxygen.

CHAPTER 1
Find Property LEADS Online

As a property investor you need leads, because leads turn into deals and deals are the only way you will make money.

Lead = potential deal

Deal = agreed sale

You need to be swimming in property leads. You can mess around thinking about property, looking online at nice houses and watching Homes Under the Hammer, or you can get serious. Serious investors educate themselves and view lots of properties – as in walking around them, and talking with the vendors and agents. The person who views the most houses wins.

I hear some uneducated investors say:

"I am just waiting for the agent to get back to me about this brilliant deal. Fingers crossed."

You should never hold out for any agent or any deal. Leave it in the pipeline but go and find more leads! I hear other uneducated investors say:

"We haven't had any properties go through yet, but everything happens for a reason."

Yes, everything happens for a reason, but the reason is usually because you messed up! Do not expect the first property you view to be the one that turns into a deal. You need to have more leads than you know what to do with. So how do you find these great property leads?

There is a magical city with all the best property leads in the world. If you learn your way around this city you will become very successful. The city is called the 'internet.'

The properties you should be viewing are Below Market Value properties.

Below Market Value (BMV) Properties

Uneducated investors claim to have found a BMV deal but really they have a BAP deal. BAP stands for Below Asking Price. It is irrelevant what the asking price is. You need to know the true current market value. On the Property Investors Crash Course, we teach you how to find the true market value of properties. This is a priceless skill, but for now just look on mouseprice.com and type in the full address for an estimate.

The way to find BMV houses is to put yourself in front of motivated sellers. The last thing you want to be is a motivated buyer. This happens by becoming emotionally attached to properties because you like them. This is a business and you should buy with your formulas, not your feelings. When emotions are high, intelligence is low. So never fall in love with a strategy or a house.

Motivated sellers are everywhere. There are millions of houses for sale in the UK right now. If only one per cent of them are highly motivated to sell, and are prepared to take a big discount, then that means there are tens of thousands of BMV properties out there today. There are many ways to find them but I will give you just two.

1) Go to gumtree.com and search for properties for sale in your area. Find the ones that have been on the market for the longest. The vendors' contact details will be at the right- hand side. Sometimes it is just an email box but usually there will be a telephone number too. These are all BMV leads.

2) Go to rightmove.co.uk and search for properties in your area, using the keyword search for phrases like motivated seller, reduced, cash only, quick sale, and see what comes up. Probably lots! If not, then search slightly further out. It does not have to be in your home town. It has to make money.

Houses of Multiple Occupancy (HMO)

Identify an area that you know has a good demand for rooms. You can find this out by asking local investors and HMO managers. Then go to spareroom.co.uk and filter the search to 'landlord ads only,' which means the landlord is managing the HMO. Scroll through the advertisements until you see a perfectly good property that has lots of rooms available. These empty rooms are probably causing the landlord much stress. The reason he or she cannot rent them out might be nothing to do with the property, but everything to do with the tired, busy landlord. The landlord's telephone number will be on the advertisement. This is an HMO lead.

Rent-to-Serviced Accommodation

Serviced accommodation allows you to rent out a property as a guest house. It has to be in the right area and does not work for every property type. When done correctly, however, it can quadruple your rentable income. One of the fastest ways to achieve high cash flow is by renting an apartment from a landlord and then legally subletting it at a much higher rate. I will explain more on this strategy later in the book, but how do you find apartments directly from the landlord?

I use a website called openrent.co.uk This is a UK site which is filled with properties to let. Nearly every one of them is available directly from the landlord. Once you've mastered and understood this serviced accommodation and the rent-to-rent strategy, anybody can find hundreds of leads in a day.

I have a saying: "*The person who views the most properties wins!*"

On one of my property training programmes, I came across a highly driven, passionate man named Anthony. He had absolutely no money, but he did have a 'whatever it takes' attitude. On the last day of the training, Anthony said:

"In the next two weeks I am going to find 40 property leads and view them all."

I knew this was an ambitious number of properties to view in such a short time and that Anthony would not achieve this. I told him that if he managed to view that many properties in just a fortnight, I would give him £1,000 to reward his efforts. The reason I did this was because I knew that in finding that many leads, and viewing that many properties, £1,000 would seem a very small amount at the end, compared to what he would be able to make from all these deals.

Sure enough, Anthony failed. I did not give him £1,000.

But also, sure enough, Anthony had sold a deal and made more than £1,000. He had also secured a 'no money down,' rent-to-rent deal which would generate a cash flow of £1,000 per month – and he managed to raise the deposit from another investor for the down payment on his first buy-to-let property.

On day one of my Financial Freedom Challenge (#FFChallenge), I simply spent the whole time ringing around estate agents and sellers. I packed my diary full of viewings for the following day. A good relationship is better than a good deal and I was excited to have spoken to a letting agent called Elena. She had landlords who were willing to let me take on their properties with a corporate let agreement in Sheffield.

I also had four HMOs to view, along with a development opportunity, in Sheffield and surrounding areas.

This was a successful day spent with my laptop in my hotel room, and all I did was exactly what I have explained in this chapter.

CHAPTER 2
Go view them and turn them into DEALS

It is possible to turn leads into deals without leaving your house. We have had many people who have found leads at the Property Investors Crash Course. They have called the seller and secured a deal. This is possible, but it is more common to clinch the deal when meeting the seller or agent in person. Also estate agents will usually only let you make an offer after a viewing. My advice is to do both. After swimming in leads, now is the time to make as many offers as you can.

I have another saying: "*The person who makes the most offers wins.*"

Thank God we live in a world of telephones, internet and cars. Imagine how difficult it would be to achieve financial freedom if we had to send letters and ride horses. Do not take such an advantage for granted because you are too scared to make a telephone call. Get over your fear of being rejected because I have seen it keep people poor and a slave to their jobs forever.

When finding BMV leads, as we learned earlier, dial the number and say:

"*Hi (name of seller) my name is _____ and I was ringing to see if your property is still for sale?*"

Assuming they say yes, continue:

"I notice it has been on the market a very long time and wondered if you knew why that might be?"

At this point they will begin to tell you their story, usually revealing their frustrations and pain points. This is when you will say:

"If I were to buy it off you tomorrow for cash, what would be the lowest you could accept but still live with?"

Then be completely silent and wait for them. In business, the person who is first to give a figure always loses. They will hopefully give a figure. At this stage, find the true market value and decide whether the discount is big enough. It is possible they will be offended and you will not get a deal. If that happens it really does not matter. You will be no poorer or weaker, and just one telephone call closer to a deal.

For a juicy BMV property deal, you need at least 15 per cent below the true market value.

You may be scared to do this because you think 'if they give me a figure and it is good, then what?'

Your problem is you are trying to work out what is going to happen down the line and what you will do next, instead of focusing on the present goal. The immediate aim is to turn a lead into a deal. Do not worry about how you are going to fund it, who you are going to sell it to, or anything else. Once they give you a figure, you can work that out then. Speaking to sellers and identifying their problems, then asking them questions, does not hold you under any obligation to buy. However, it puts you in a position where you have a deal.

When texting tired HMO landlords, write something simple such as:

"Hey (name). I have seen your rooms for rent. Would you consider selling the property or receiving a monthly guaranteed rent? If so, I would love to talk.

Regards, (your name)."

If you only send three text messages, you probably will not get a response. During my #FFChallenge I sent over 100 messages like this in all surrounding areas.

I also rang the owner of every apartment on the market in Sheffield (Sheffield was my selected location pulled from a hat) and managed to book three viewings the following day.

I did not waste time viewing apartments unless I knew the landlord was happy with me agreeing a corporate let on the property and running it as rent-to-rent/serviced accommodation.

I simply said:

"Hi, I am ringing about (name the property). Is it still available?"

If the owner replies yes, continue:

"I could potentially take it on as a corporate let. This would mean my company would pay the full rent over a three to five-year period. We would then let our guests stay there through Booking.com Is this something you're familiar with?"

Sometimes at this point the agent or landlord will not be interested. In which case, fine! Other times they will be open to this type of arrangement. Excellent!

Your purpose should not be to calculate every minor detail at this juncture. You could spend hours working out the figures on an apartment, only for the agent to say:

"Sorry we don't do corporate lets."

The key is to get in front of as many open-minded agents and motivated sellers as possible. Finding a good relationship is far better than a good deal.

We had a mother and daughter named Leah and Sheryl attend our Property Investors Crash Course. Shortly afterwards they found an agent who was willing to pass onto them city centre apartments for serviced accommodation. From this one agent, the mother and daughter are making a monthly profit of £14,000. If you want to hear their full story, just search on YouTube for Financially Free in 6 WEEKS! | Winners on a Wednesday #7.

When buying properties, always make an offer that is specific. This makes it look like your offer has been well thought out and you will not increase it. If it is on for £100,000 and you offer £80,000, the owner may say:

"*Meet me in the middle at £90,000.*"

However, if it is on for £100,000 and you offer £81,750, he or she will often say:

"*Let's round it up to £82,000.*"

It is odd, but it works. If the owner accepts first time round, it means you offered too high. Somebody once said:

"*If you are not embarrassed by your offer, it is not low enough.*"

I use a clever technique when offering on properties that I call 'if … would.'
An example of this would be,

"*If I were to offer you £81,750, would you accept?*"

When you do this, one of two things will happen:

1) The person will say '*yes.*' In which case, you have not officially offered. You just said: "*If I were to offer ….*" This then gives you time to say:

"*Excellent, well I should be able to do that. Just give me a couple days to confirm.*"

2) The reply is no. In which case, you can ask:

"Well, what would you accept then?"

When you are given the price, always negotiate, continuing to use the 'if . . . would' strategy.

You can always come back and say no. Never make a formal offer that you cannot commit to on the basis that you hope to sell it.

Once you have a soft agreement – in other words, you know what the owner would accept because you have identified his or her pain point and made an 'if . . . would' offer – you can get to work on crunching the numbers and deciding if this will definitely work. Do not waste your time intensively calculating the numbers if you have no idea what they would accept. Do not bother working out the XYZ before you have walked the ABC. When watching a movie you do not watch the end first to decide if you want to watch it. You take a slight gamble and watch it from the beginning. In the same way, you do not know exactly what is going to happen with your deals, in your business and with your life. Just put one foot in front of the other until you get there. If you have not done so already, a great first step would be joining me at the Property Investors Crash Course where you will learn to formulate and understand the difference between a good and a bad deal.

On day two of my #FFChallenge, I managed to find five deals. They were:

Three rent-to-rent serviced apartments in Sheffield that would cost me approximately £2,500 each to cover the first month's rent, deposit and agent fees. This would total £7,500 but I would be making around £1,000 per month on each one. So they were extremely juicy deals.

One HMO in Doncaster which I agreed to purchase at £149,000 was being rented out for £2,000 a month. The owners were selling the property due to a divorce. It would yield me a return on investment (ROI) of over 20 per cent. Whilst I did not have any money to buy the house, I planned to sell this deal for £2,500 to an investor who had the money in place.

A development opportunity in Doncaster was on the market at £97,000. I offered £96,750 and was asked to round it up. It was worth £120,000 based on my advanced calculations, so I was delighted with this deal. Even better, it had the opportunity to be converted into two flats which would lift the value even more and produce an ROI of at least 17 per cent. Sadly, I did not have any money to buy it, but I planned to also sell this deal for £2,500.

If I was able to sell the development opportunity for £2,500 and the HMO for £2,500, this would give me enough money to secure two of the rent-to-rents. They in turn would give me a passive monthly income of £2,000.

CHAPTER 3
Find Investors and Build Your Network

The property business is a people business. Ultimately all of your money is going to come from people, not property. Property is simply your product, but the money will come from your customers. Your customers will be tenants and property buyers. Most people think that the most valuable commodity in property investing is money. This is completely wrong. The most important commodity is actually knowledge, followed by network. During my challenge, not only did I not have access to my own money, I was not allowed to tap into my network. I could only do business with strangers. I am known for stating:

"I would rather lose all of my money than lose all of my network."

At this moment I had lost both. When buying property these are typically the key players you need in your power team:

S. olicitor
A. ccountant
M. ortgage broker
U. (you)
E. state agent
L. abourer

Your solicitor will take care of the legal side of the business and deal with the completion of your property. The accountant will advise you whether you need a company, or if it is better to buy as an individual, and then make sure you are paying as little tax as possible by claiming expenses properly. A mortgage broker will get you the best rates on your mortgage loans and find the most suitable lenders. You are the biggest player in your power team as you will personally have to oversee all the different departments and ensure everybody is doing their job properly. The estate and letting agent will deal with the tenants and manage the everyday running of your portfolio. The labourers will deal with maintenance, renovations or general dogsbody jobs, depending on your criteria. However, on this occasion I had no money and was not buying any properties. My plan was to sell properties to make some quick cash, and then to use it to secure rent-to-rent deals that would give me a great monthly cash flow. Therefore, my biggest need was to find some investors who might be open to paying me a sourcing fee.

The best way to build your investor list from scratch is to go to networking events. That is why on the evening of day two, as soon as I arrived back to my hotel after all the viewings and securing all the deals, I went online to search for some networking events and property meetings. There were surprisingly fewer than I had thought there would be, but after much searching I found a two-day property training programme in Birmingham. It was free to attend which was ideal as I had no money.

To build your investor list you can do it virtually online. The fastest way, however, to build trust is in person. I would recommend going to a property networking event, a business networking event, or anything you can find where there will be people open to investing in property. I have some students who go to auctions and then approach the investors who got outbid to tell them about their packaged deals. Genius!

When I arrived at the property meeting, I was wearing a wig and fake glasses to make me unrecognisable. The worst thing you can do is be pushy with your deals, especially to complete strangers that do not know you from Adam. You will only look desperate and push people away. For this reason I decided not to sell any deals at all that day. People will only buy from you when they know you, like you and trust you. I had one day to build trust with investors and show them that I knew my stuff! My strategy was to identify the serious investors by asking them questions. The kind of questions I would ask might be:

"What are you here for?" "How long have you been in property?" "What sort of deals are you looking to buy?"

I sat with as many investors as possible over lunch and coffee breaks, listening to their stories. I offered help and advice to people who were undecided on their strategy. This demonstrated to them that I was an expert, and they began to trust and respect me. I told them I was new to property myself, but had spent a lot of time going to training programmes and networking with good property players. This intrigued them and I slowly became popular as the day progressed. I went by the name Lucas Ruby. Before the challenge began I had registered Lucas Ruby LTD with Companies House and set up a bank account, as well as a compliant company. To sell deals you do need to be complaint which is quite straightforward and inexpensive (for more details read Whatever It Takes by Alasdair Cunningham).

I met one guy named Saj Hussain. I knew Saj already as he is a well-respected investor from Birmingham, but he did not see through my cheap disguise. After a long conversation with him, and him telling me he was actively building his portfolio, I said:

"Saj, I have a few really good deals I am looking to sell. If the figures worked for you, would you be interested in buying one from me?"

Saj said he was not interested in anything too far from Birmingham. I could have left it at that, but the fact that Saj now had a relationship with me was paramount. In the same way that you leverage your money by getting the bank to give you a mortgage, you can leverage your network. The average person knows 1,000 people. At this meeting there were only about 60 people in the room, but I was seeing 60,000 people because I know the power of leverage. I said to Saj:

"I appreciate you are only looking in Birmingham and these deals are around Sheffield. Who do you know who would benefit from seeing these deals I have?"

Saj went through his telephone book and gave me the details of another influential property investor. All this time he had no idea I was Samuel Leeds. I rang his contact and built instant trust by saying:

"Hello I am a friend of Saj's. I was with him just today and he said I should call you about a deal I have. Are you free to speak?"

This particular lead did not come to anything, but I was doing this all day. I spent the whole day collecting business cards, taking people's details and asking for referrals. By the time I got home I put all of my new contacts onto a spreadsheet and set up a customer relations management (CRM) system. This is a database of everybody you know and you can email them all at once. I used mailchimp.com because it is free. I stayed up until the early hours of the morning and even made a website on wix.com which also cost me £0.00. The website was lucasruby.com

It was only day three of my #FFChallenge and I was now known and respected by dozens of property investors – and had deals to sell.

CHAPTER 4
Package Your Deals and Sell Them to Investors

On day four my car broke down on the motorway. Forced to abandon it and scrounge a lift, I arrived at the property meeting with my suitcase and belongings in plastic carrier bags. I was losing focus and beginning to panic about finding the money for these deals. I was heartened, though, by the warm welcome I received from all my new friends and several said:

"Lucas, I want to talk to you about one of your property deals."

I started to get excited again. If I sold just two deals for £2,500 each, that would give me enough to secure two serviced apartments generating around £2,000 per month. I was determined to make that happen.

There were three people who were very hot. Hot in this context means they are ready to buy. When selling deals, here are the steps to take:

Present your Property

You have to present your property and demonstrate it is a packaged deal. You have to show all of the figures and have a clear breakdown of the numbers. This is something we teach you at the Property

Investors Crash Course as it is crucial you can calculate and present the return on investment.

If the property is on the internet, you need to make sure the potential investor cannot find it and cut you out of the loop. The way around this is to either exclude the full address from the details, or make the individual sign a non-disclosure agreement (NDA). This means he or she cannot disclose the information or go directly to the seller.

This presentation should be written and sent via an email. It should include the condition of the property, the achievable rent, proof of the true market value, agreed purchase price and any other relevant information. At the bottom of the email, make sure you tell the investor how much your fee will be and how to reserve the property. I asked the person to just call me to reserve it and added it was on a first come, first served basis. This creates a little bit of urgency and of course is 100 per cent true.

Ask Questions

Once you have emailed this presentation to your list of investors, you will no doubt begin getting calls. It is vitally important that when investors ring, you remain in control. The person who asks the most questions is the person who is in control.

Untrained property sellers often spend hours on the telephone answering 21 questions about the deal, only for the investor to then say:

"I will think about it," or *"I will speak to my wife and get back to you in three years' time,"* or *"let me consult my lawyer and my dog."*

The key is to ask them the questions. The first question I always ask is:

"What was it that you liked about this property?"

This forces the investor to sell himself to the property, so that I don't have to. He is just reminding himself why he called me, and convincing himself to buy it.

Once he (or she) has told me what he likes about it, I am the one in control. I will then say and ask:

"I have lots of investors to phone about this property, so would it be ok if I ask some questions to check it might be suitable for you?"

This again creates a sense of urgency for the person. I am not manipulating the investor. I am just making it easy for him to buy. The bottom line is he called me because he wants the property. The deal is good. It is the ethical thing now to pre-qualify him to make sure he is right for it. In doing this, it shows you are not desperate for the money but are truly trying to serve him, and inadvertently will make him really want to buy. Win win! If he begins to try to take control and start asking me lots of questions, I will answer them but then immediately follow with another question, such as:

"Have you got a mortgage in principle?" "Have you got the funds in place to go?" "Is this your first property?"

Close

Once the investor has answered yes to the pre-qualifying questions, I usually say:

"Well it sounds like you are a good fit for the property. Shall I just run through the key points of the deal once more before we talk about the next steps?"

At this point you are telling him what is about to happen. Namely, you will go back over everything he already knows and summarise it, ready to move to the next steps. He will like the fact you are taking control because, if he wants the property, it shows your confidence and certainty.

Once you have summarised, it is time to give him a final chance to ask any pressing questions. He may ask genuine questions, or he may begin to ask trivial questions about the colour of the front door. If he has no more questions, you have a deal. If he does have questions, you need to answer each question with a pre-close.

Most people hate being closed because it means they actually have to make a decision. I love being closed because I like making decisions. If you do not like being sold to, it means you do not like selling, and if you do not like selling, it means you are broke! If you want to get on in life you better get good at closing deals. If it makes you feel uncomfortable then get over it. You can either be comfortable and broke, or uncomfortable and rich.

At the Property Investors Crash Course people step so far out of their comfort zone and that is what gets them the results. I am known for saying:

"If you are not growing, you are dying, and the only way to grow is outside of your comfort zone. So it's time to get comfortable being uncomfortable."

By now you have an investor who has said he really likes the deal. He is ready to buy and he has the funds in place. He is now asking nominal questions simply because he is a human being playing for time. The reason he is doing that is he does not like making decisions. Your job to best serve him is to sell him the deal. So for every question you answer you will ask him a pre-close question, such as:

"If you were to go ahead, how soon would you be able to pay the reservation fee?"

"If I can verify everything I've just said over an email, would you like to go ahead?"

You will notice these are also 'if . . . would' questions like we used earlier for negotiating the deal in the first place. You will use these magic words all the time as a successful property entrepreneur.

If he answers positively to the pre-close, you need to just assume he is good to go. Do not talk too much.

Just ask these questions. Let him sell himself and then move to the next phase.

Terms and Conditions

You should never do business without a clear written agreement. This is not only to prevent people from lying and going back on their verbal word, but also for clarification because human beings are known to forget. Even when I do business with my relatives, I always make sure everything is written down clearly. I completely trust them, but I have been in this game long enough to know its importance.

At this point in the conversation, you are going to tell the investor exactly what is going to happen.

"I am delighted you would like to secure the property. Here is what happens now. I will send you over a contract with our terms and conditions. As soon as you've read these and are happy, sign them and send them back. I will then promptly invoice you our bank details for the £2,500 finder's fee, and once this is paid the property will be reserved for you. I will then introduce you to the seller and management company, and your solicitor will take over from there. Is that all ok?"

Get the buyer to agree on time frames because you do not want to be waiting around for days to get paid. You can get your contracts drawn up inexpensively by a solicitor, or you can just write out your own terms in plain English yourself. As long as they are fair and in keeping with the law, they will stand up in court, even if they are just contained in an email dialogue with no signed contract. I know because I have personally sold over 250 properties and have trained hundreds of deal packagers – and have seen everything. I am not a lawyer and cannot advise on legal matters, but it is imperative you are set up compliantly to cover yourself. You can discover this yourself in our further training or read about it in Whatever It Takes by Alasdair Cunningham.

Invoice

When the investor returns the agreed terms and conditions, it is time to send the invoice. While I was Lucas Ruby, I used an invoice app on my telephone called Invoice2Go which sends professional invoices in seconds and takes minutes to set up.

I regularly tell my students:

"They have not been sold, until you see the gold."

In other words, do not celebrate the sale until you have the money in your bank. I always suggest to never rely on anybody and to keep trying to sell the deal until somebody pays. This has to be a first come, first served arrangement. The investor has not truly reserved it until he pays the fee. At times I have sent three people an invoice all at a similar time and occasionally more than one person will send the money. This is brilliant when it happens because you just have to refund the person who was the slowest, keeping the fastest investor's money. The slow one will be ready to buy the next deal and over time you will have a list of ready-to-go investors. Your first deal is always the hardest. However, when you have done it once you will get confident and skilled. The whole process will also become extremely exhilarating and enormously profitable.

Expectations

Make sure you set the right expectations with your investors and never exaggerate the figures to make them more attractive to sell. In property things can occasionally go wrong but you do not want unhappy investors. I strongly recommend only selling deals you would buy yourself under the right circumstances. Make sure too that your investors understand your terms and conditions. Even if they sign the terms, they may have misunderstood them. You will win the court case, if there is one, but may get bad reviews, which is not worth it. I am not perfect. I have dropped the ball at times over the last ten years, but the reason I have managed to become a multi-millionaire is because I have a nationwide reputation to always under promise and over deliver in everything I do.

Sadly, towards the end of day four of my #FFChallenge the event organisers noticed I had a microphone and was secretly recording, so I got kicked out. If you want to see it happen, then just search for the documentary on YouTube called Undercover Millionaire Starts Again From Scratch - FINANCIAL FREEDOM CHALLENGE.

CHAPTER 5
Use the Money to Build Your Own Portfolio

Building your own portfolio is a smart thing to do alongside deal packaging. It is not a bad idea to focus on one strategy, but at the same time you do not want all your eggs in one basket. Your portfolio can consist of rent-to-rent, lease options, buy-to-let and HMOs but it really depends on your personal goals. Many of my students begin with deal packaging because not only is it one of the quickest ways to generate fast cash, but it forces you to become an excellent property finder. This means that you can keep the very best ones for yourself and get paid to do it. Alasdair Cunningham came to the Property Investors Crash Course and decided to focus on deal packaging. He now makes £25,000 per month from just passing deals onto investors. That would be enough for a down payment to buy a £100,000 property every single month!

You may wonder why I keep referring to so many of my students. It is because I am so eager for you to realise that I am not superhuman. I am not the only person who has managed to become financially free using these strategies. There are thousands of others in the UK who have done it and I have helped hundreds first-hand. I interview a new success student on my YouTube channel every single week and most of them are very ordinary people, all from completely different backgrounds.

Paul and Ann Waters do not like dealing with investors. They are great at finding properties but they prefer to deal with motivated sellers than sell deals to the investors. Since coming on the crash course the first time round, which was about 18 months ago, they have made over £50,000 in sourcing fees, yet have never sold a deal and have no investors on their list. All they do is pass on their deals to a sourcer who then sells the deal for them and they split the fee. Paul and Ann have used the money to buy their own property in Grimsby. With the £50,000 they bought a cheap property, refurbished it and then refinanced it, pulling nearly all of the £50,000 back out to do it again. Their story was so successful that it made headlines in the Grimsby Telegraph, despite them living in East Sussex.

The average deal sells for about £2,500, so selling one deal per week would add up to about £10,000 per month. Ironically this would just about be enough for a deposit on a £40,000 house each month. What is to stop you doing this immediately? Maybe buying a property each month sounds ambitious, but you do not need to sell many properties to quit your job. Passing on one deal per month would replace the average salary. Now that is achievable.

Your first deal is always your hardest. Thereafter it gets easier and easier. Lucas Ruby was having serious trouble managing to sell any of his superb deals and the agents were beginning to get impatient. The HMO estate agent was chasing me for my documents, as was the agent for the development opportunity. I was meeting Elena later that morning to pay her £4,850 to secure two of my serviced apartments. The problem was that I did not have any money at all, and I had not sold any deals yet.

It was frustrating because Samuel Leeds could sell it within 30 seconds, but Lucas Ruby just did not have the credibility to pull it off. Elena had also asked me to bring my photo ID and my pay slips to show my company could afford the rent for the landlord. When I got to her office, I did not have the money and I was not in a position to let her credit check me because Lucas Ruby had no credit nor job. I explained that my company was new and I did not have any income before the business was set up due to being a university student. The agent had no idea I was actually an undercover millionaire.

I do not remember exactly what I said, although part of the conversation is on the YouTube documentary. She told me not to worry about the finances, as long as I was confident I could pay the rent on time, and provide my ID and proof of address. My referee said it was 'unbelievable luck.' I say 'the more I practise the luckier I get.' The alternative would have been to find a guarantor. This would have been challenging for Lucas as he did not have any family.

I asked Elena:

"Can I make a bank transfer on my laptop?"

She responded:

"That's fine. Here are the bank details. You can do it now in the office."

In that moment I had no choice but to make a pretend payment. I said the money had left my account but I had not actually sent anything because I did not have a penny to my name. She said as soon as it landed she would call me and arrange for me to go back to collect the two sets of keys. It felt so close, but yet so far away, and I was beginning to feel anxious.

A few hours later she was ringing me asking what was going on as she had not received the payment. I honestly thought I was going to lose the apartments and did not have anything to tell her.

That same evening I attended a networking event where unfortunately my cover was blown because people recognised me from my voice, despite the fake tan, glasses and wig. People began to queue up to take selfies and I realised I could not sell any deal at that event as they knew who I was. While driving home that evening I had a conversation with a gentleman named Sean who been referred to me from somebody I met at the two-day property meeting. Using the sales techniques learned in the previous chapter, I managed to get him to commit to buying the development opportunity but he said he wanted to pay the following day. Whilst I was delighted I knew:

"If you haven't got the gold, they haven't been sold."

It is possible to sell lots of deals, make lots of money, use that money to buy properties and then let the snowball grow and grow until you become a millionaire. However, never forget that your first deal is extremely hard. Even as Samuel Leeds, with all my knowledge, confidence and experience, I was really struggling.

CHAPTER 6
Utilise 'No Money Down' Strategies such as R2Rs and LOAs

I woke up on day six of my Financial Freedom Challenge to a text message from an investor, Raj, who wanted to secure my Doncaster HMO. I was over the moon! I sent him the terms and he agreed to pay £2,500 later that day. I needed precisely £4,850 to secure two of my serviced apartments and now had two buyers who were promising to pay a total of £5,000.

I spent the morning calling all my investors and using all my sales skills as though my life depended on it. I spoke to a lady called Pam about a third serviced apartment that was also in Sheffield. I told her I was getting two apartments in the same area and she could use the same management systems I was choosing for my own flats. I also gave her a three-month break clause so that she could pull out after this period and I would refund her. I knew, of course, this would not happen but I needed to give her complete peace of mind because Lucas Ruby did not have the reputation and trust that Samuel Leeds enjoys.

Once I ran out of people to ring, I could have waited for money to come in and spent my time worrying about paying Elena and what to say to delay the agents. But I knew that would not get me anywhere. And anyway they probably had other things to think about besides chasing me. Instead I got out my laptop and started to find more leads. This time I was looking for a lease option agreement (LOA) which is when you buy a house but agree with the seller to pay for the property down the line. This is usually some years down the line. In the meantime you benefit from the capital appreciation of the property and, of course, the rent. LOAs are among my favourite kind of deals because I have got very wealthy from them as Samuel Leeds over the past ten years.

While I was booking viewings and speaking to sellers, I had an email with the signed terms and a message from Raj saying:

"*Your fee has been paid!*"

I immediately checked my Lucas Ruby bank account and there it was: £2,500!!!! It felt like such a large amount of money, and yet I cannot remember the last time I got so excited about such a small amount. The good news was I had £2,500 in my bank. The bad news was I needed £4,850 as soon as possible. I went on travelling across the country in a car that was bright yellow, 15 years old and completely falling apart. I viewed properties in Sheffield, Doncaster and Hull. I offered to buy some properties on a lease option agreement and had vendors who were very interested. Nothing to date has come from those viewings but to learn more about lease options you can watch the interview of one of my successful students, Ian Pattison, who has dozens of them:

Towards the end of the day, as I was walking back towards my battered car, I felt the urge to check my bank account again. I could not believe it. There was £5,000 in there. Sean had now also paid for his development opportunity. I did the most ludicrous celebration dance that sadly made it into the documentary. I sat in the car and paid £4,850 to Elena. I also collected all the documents from Raj and Sean, and forwarded them to the estate agents. Elena had received the money and agreed for me to get the keys the next day. The breakdown of the £4,850 looked like this:

Apartment 1 (two-bed furnished apartment)

£1,300 - two months' upfront rent of £650
£650   - refundable deposit
£200   - application fee to agent

Apartment 2 (four-bed part-furnished penthouse)

£1,250 - one month's rent
£1,250 - refundable deposit
£200   - application fee to agent

Total required to secure the two apartments on a rent-to-rent basis: £4,850

How will I manage these serviced apartments?

Managing serviced apartments is an absolute nightmare if you do not have good systems in place.

I would highly recommend speaking to a good property training company, such as ours, before setting up a serviced accommodation property because you can lose thousands of pounds and hundreds of hours doing it incorrectly. Here is a brief checklist of what you need to do:

1) Advertise

After securing the two apartments I was so excited I wanted to see the money coming in as soon as possible, so I put it up myself on Airbnb and Booking.com in a frantic rush.
Usually my team deals with this side of the business. I am not an expert in listing online properties and I am not going to lie, I did it all wrong! The pictures were terrible, the description was bad, and there was no online calendar that synced all the bookings together to avoid double bookings. The rates were also all the same when you should vary them dramatically depending on the day and the season. I did get bookings coming in quickly but double bookings started happening and my listings were generally so poor my team removed them and relisted them properly. I could have done it myself if I had had the time. But after finishing my challenge I went to Dubai and it was just the last thing I wanted to do whilst lying on one of the most breathtaking beaches in the world.

2) Key Systems

The worst thing you can ever do is let the guests in yourself as this will then just become a job. The easiest way to make this happen is by putting a key safe outside, I use one called KeyMaster that can be installed easily and purchased for around £17 from Argos or Screwfix. In the confirmation email that guests receive it will also inform them of the key safe and the code. I like to do a brief video showing them where it is. You can alternatively use companies like KeyNest if the property does not allow for a key safe outside.

3) Cleaners

The cleaners are your best asset, so choose carefully. The cleaners will go to the property each time a new guest leaves. They will not only clean it, but make sure everything is in order and change over the bed sheets/covers. I would recommend using a company that understands exactly what you need, rather than a self-employed individual who could let you down.

4) Virtual PA

There will be times when the cleaner, guests or the landlord will need to speak to you. Sometimes this will be urgent such as the guests not being able to find the property. If you give everybody your personal number this will mean it will never be true passive income. My advice would be to do it yourself first time around for just a few months. Understand the processes and systems inside out. When you get a problem or a question, write the answer in a notebook. You will notice the same questions keep coming up again and again. Once you know every question that could crop up that is when you find a 24/7 virtual PA company such as alldayPA. Tell the operators all the answers and let them give the answers. If they do not know the answers themselves, they will email you. You can reply and then add that to the notepad. Over time, this will become a high cash-flowing business that is completely hands-off.

How much am I making from these two SA apartments?

I am making at best £2,650 per month, at worst £1,000 per month, or in the most likely case, £1,500 per month.

Until you have been running them for at least one year, but ideally several years, you cannot know 100 per cent what the exact earnings will be. This is because serviced accommodation is a business that will vary each month depending on many factors. You just need to make sure the worst case scenario will not cripple you. If you do not know the market well, you should always have a break clause after three or six months with the landlord. As I write this it is only six weeks after securing the apartments, but I have had many bookings and the guests have loved the apartments so far. It will usually take some months to build up good reviews which then snowball into more bookings. Remember, this is a business. Much more important than how the apartments are performing is how my relationships with the agents are faring. I have since had half a dozen more no money down opportunities passed to me by the agents who I found as Lucas Ruby.

Although I did need funds to secure these deals, I started the #FFChallenge with nothing but made that money during the week. Therefore, anybody can do this regardless of your current financial situation. We even have international students who live overseas securing these type of deals in the UK. Check out the YouTube video entitled - Investing in UK Property from OVERSEAS | Winners on a Wednesday #11.

I have lost count of the number of people who have attended my crash course and then replaced their income with lease option agreements and rent-to-rent deals. Just visit my website and see the hundreds of stories: www.property-investors.co.uk

Do lease options stand up in court? Yes. I have been in this business long enough to have bought properties at the end of the lease at embarrassingly low prices.

Is serviced accommodation the way forward? You have to know what you are doing when taking on such a property because there are some laws and rules that you need to comply with. The properties also have to be in the right area and you need to have the right booking systems in place.

Do not attempt to do this without support and professional paid-for training. You would not drive a car without lessons and passing your test, or attempt surgery before qualifying as a doctor. This is a business not to be taken lightly. You can expect powerful results but you will not get rich quickly. It is more like: get educated and then get wealthy over a period of time.

Hopefully in this book you have already learned how to find leads, make deals, build your network, sell deals, build your portfolio and buy properties without using any money. There is, however, one more crucial ingredient.

CHAPTER 7
Take Massive Action and Do Not Be Afraid of What Anybody Thinks

My decision to start all over again on camera was a brave one. I could have failed and looked ridiculous. Many people were hoping I would fail just to give them an excuse to fail. I had no control over the editing of the video as it was done by a third-party freelancer, Jan Rekelhof, who was determined to find the truth about whether the challenge was really possible. My reputation was on the line and this could have resulted in my name being a laughing stock in the property industry for many years to come.

I have a saying: - "*Big risk is big reward.*"

There is always a reason you cannot be successful. There is also always a reason you can and why you should be. You get to decide which reasons you live by and you get to create your own life. All of the successes that came from my seven days on the #FFChallenge came with a risk that I would fail or get rejected. The best things in life are on the other side of fear. So, if you are reading this but are coming up with excuses already as to why now is 'not the right time,' I am telling you it is! There will never be a perfect time. Your time is today.

On day seven, I went and collected the keys to my two serviced apartments. My car would not start that morning so I took a bus. While I was on the bus I received a payment from Pam for £3,000. I had officially made £8,000 in seven days. I told Elena who I really was and gave her my real Samuel Leeds ID. She was gobsmacked! She had never heard of Samuel Leeds but went straight to Google to find out if I was legitimate.

Elena and I have become friends and she even shared the documentary on her Facebook wall. She has agreed to pass on many more apartments and even better deals to Lucas. In being prepared to look stupid in front of Elena, I actually gained an excellent business contact and a new friend. Most people live a boring life because they are afraid to look stupid in front of other people who would not even attend their funeral.

I believe life is too short to worry about looking silly. If you have the ability to potentially make a lot of money, but do not do so because of laziness or fear, I would call that selfish. People love to make property so complicated just to stop you doing it, because they are afraid themselves. But being a property entrepreneur is actually very easy and financial freedom is very possible.

After completing my #FFChallenge in just seven days, I was surprised it was achieved so quickly and so I surprised my beautiful wife, Amanda, with a luxurious holiday in Dubai for two weeks. It was an incredible feeling lying on the beach while watching my iPhone ping every few hours with a new booking for my Sheffield apartment. The average booking is £120 per night per apartment and the average occupancy rate in Sheffield for serviced accommodation is currently around 80 per cent. I expect to make around £2,000 per month for these apartments, and Elena is going to pass me plenty more. I also had £3,000 left over to play with at the end of the week.

In the space of a fortnight, the #FFChallenge has had over half a million views on YouTube and yesterday I was a guest on the BBC Midlands Today programme. I was interviewed live on the teatime news.

The big risk of documenting this challenge paid off with a big reward, namely proving to the world that financial freedom is possible for anyone.

Admittedly, I had a huge advantage because of my previous property experience, but anybody can freely acquire this knowledge. I would like to invite you to begin your education as a property investor by joining me now at the Property Investors Crash Course.

Property is the second-best investment you can make. The best investment is in yourself.

Congratulations on reading this book, but participation is the only way to truly know something. Therefore, it is time for you to learn the rules of the game and then play to win. The most dangerous individuals are motivated idiots. The fact you have read this book suggests you are motivated to become financially free. I urge you to invest in yourself to turn this desire into a reality.

Join me for free at the Property Investors Crash Course and be one of the hundreds of other success students smashing their own #FFChallenge. It could be the best present you could ever receive.

Claim FREE Ticket at
www.property-investors.co.uk

Thank you so much for your support,
Samuel Leeds AKA Lucas Ruby

The following articles about the Financial Freedom Challenge were featured in newspapers all over the UK

Produced by Enigma Communications

Property tycoon dons wig and fake glasses in undercover mission to prove you don't need money to succeed

He drove off in an old banger, had an empty bank account and a week later was even able to hand a homeless charity £2,000 from his dealings

A Lichfield property tycoon took just a week to become financially free again after 10,000 people on social media challenged him to leave town and build his portfolio from scratch with no money.

Multi-millionaire Samuel Leeds drove a 'dodgy old banger' to a hotel which had been pre-booked for him in a city he didn't know. With an empty bank account, a zero-credit rating and no access to any funds – he had to make money in seven days or face eviction.

Towards the end of the trip Samuel had spent the £50 he was allowed for essentials and had not eaten for a day. But right on the wire he earned £8,000 from selling property deals to investors and was able to secure two luxury apartments, generating a monthly profit of £2,000.

The 27-year-old entrepreneur even had enough cash left over to stop off in Manchester on his way home and hand out £2,000 to a homeless charity.

To succeed under the rules of the *Financial Freedom Challenge,* Samuel had to make a minimum of £3,000 – at least half of which had to be in the form of an ongoing passive income.

Wearing a black wig and false glasses, he went under the alias of Lucas Ruby. His battered 12-year-old Scimitar nearly put the brakes on the challenge when it broke down twice and eventually had to be abandoned.

While Samuel was allowed to travel freely, he had to sleep in the same hotel each night. All dealings had to be conducted with strangers and the entire trip was documented by a videographer. The results were later checked by two independent experts from the worlds of finance and property.

The young businessman is a committed Christian who runs Property Investors UK, based at Hilton Hall in Essington. As one of the country's top property trainers, he has taught thousands of people how to achieve financial independence through buying and renting out houses. By the time he was 21 he was wealthy enough to retire.

During 2018 alone, Samuel invested in 27 properties and was featured in newspapers and on TV when he bought Ribbesford House in Worcestershire, one of Britain's most historic homes. He also runs a Christian networking business underpinned by the ethos that accumulating riches can be a force for good if it also benefits others. His company has raised thousands of pounds for charities at home and overseas. Remarkably, he took on the challenge just months after shattering his kneecap in Uganda while on a trip to bring fresh water to remote villages. He had an emergency operation and was told he might not walk properly again but has largely recovered.

The entrepreneur's mantra has always been that anyone with the right knowledge can make money through property investing – even if they are strapped for cash. His challenge was about proving that.

Sheffield was chosen as the destination after the steel city was randomly picked out of a hat in front of a live audience.

Samuel described the trip as both exhilarating and traumatic.

"I was unceremoniously thrown out of two business events and even had my hidden microphone removed. At one time I thought I might have to sleep in the car or on the street to continue the challenge. I was under so much pressure to succeed and save face. But if I can achieve what I did in a week with no money to invest, just imagine what's possible in a year!"

Samuel got down to work moments after checking into his hotel. He was up until the early hours, trawling Rightmove, Gumtree, OpenRent and SpareRoom for potential investment properties. The second day was spent viewing homes on his shortlist, including some new city centre apartments owned by a wealthy property developer.

"The £650 monthly rent seemed reasonable to me, so I offered to pay him the full amount, so long as he agreed to me sub-letting the accommodation and installing key safes outside. I knew that by putting the properties on the likes of Airbnb, and Booking.com they would achieve between £120 and £200 a night. I had the potential to make a healthy profit and the landlord was still getting the rent he wanted."

Samuel shook hands on a deal to take over two of the apartments, plus a penthouse suite. The plan was to keep two and sell the penthouse deal to an investor. He had also identified two other rental properties with multiple rooms, which he was confident would earn him a significant 'finders' fee.' The money raised from selling on the three deals would cover the deposit/advance rent on the two apartments, netting him a monthly profit of £2,000.

However, he soon found out that selling deals at networking events as the unknown Lucas Ruby was no easy task.

"It was so frustrating to find investors were hesitant because the figures I was offering stacked up. My terms and conditions also meant that purchasers were protected if anything I said turned out not to be the case.

"I even had one potential investor tell me he was looking to pay £200,000 for a property that would yield £1,500 a month in rent. I told him I had found a property available at half that money which would make the same profit. All I wanted was a fee of £2,500, but he just kept saying I don't know you."

At another property network meeting, Samuel decided to win confidence by demonstrating his knowledge.

"I introduced myself as a deal sourcer and just mentioned I had a couple of interesting properties. I didn't do any hard selling in the room. I just concentrated on giving people sound advice and earning their trust. About half a dozen people wanted to know more about my deals, and I said I would bring them more information the next day."

Unfortunately, Samuel's car broke down when he tried to return. He arrived by bus, too late to see the people who had expressed interest in his deals. However, Lucas was gaining more respect, with several other investors prepared to entrust him with their money. With success in his grasp, the event organisers suddenly became suspicious after spotting his microphone. He was asked to leave, with the gathering told Lucas 'is not who he says he is.'

Samuel's stress levels rose even further when the estate agent for the apartments asked him to make the first payment.

"I just didn't know how to handle that one. I ended up taking out my laptop at their offices and shamefully saying the money had been transferred. It bought me a little extra time, but soon afterwards I got a call saying nothing had been received."

Just when eviction from his hotel looked inevitable Samuel struck gold. He had sent a mass email out to all the people he had met in Sheffield, and to many contacts they had suggested to him.

"That day I sold the deals for two multi-let properties and the penthouse apartment for £8,000. I was able to pay the agent the £4,850 for the deposits and advanced rents to secure the two other apartments for myself. I was also able to rent some attractive furniture.

"The estate agents and investors were amazed when I revealed I was an undercover property multi-millionaire. They googled my name straightaway and thought it was incredible."

On the way home, a jubilant Samuel headed to Manchester to present a cheque to Sid Williams, founder of the Embassy charity which provides a sanctuary for the homeless.

"Hundreds of people in the UK die each year as a result of being out in the cold. Sid acquired a former tour bus used by bands like Coldplay and lets homeless people sleep on it while he helps to secure council houses for them. He said the £2,000 I gave him would pay for 95 sleeps off the street and could save lives."

With a few hundred pounds left, Samuel remembered the help given to him by a Good Samaritan when his car broke down:

"A mechanic called Tony came out and must have thought Lucas Ruby was really struggling for money. He fixed my banger for free at a time when I had virtually run out of cash.

"I called the garage and they told me he had just smashed his mobile phone. I used the remaining money to buy Tony a new Samsung along with some cinema tickets."

Samuel had one final surprise up his sleeve. Having finished the challenge early he was able to book a holiday in Dubai with his wife Amanda.

"We have a beautiful daughter Ruby and Amanda is expecting our little boy in January. We haven't seen as much of each other as we would have liked recently.

"The challenge enabled me to practice what I preach. Even if you haven't got any money you can become successful in property, so long as you have the knowledge, and, no matter how successful you become, you should always make time for the most important people in your life."

*The documentary of Samuel's *Financial Freedom Challenge* is now available for viewing on his YouTube channel and is attracting thousands of views per day.

Samuel with wife Amanda and daughter Ruby shortly before leaving his Lichfield home to take on the Financial Freedom Challenge.

Samuel, in disguise as Lucas Ruby, calls for assistance after his makeshift car broke down.

Founder of homeless bus charity left stunned as his prayers for £2,000 are instantly answered

Handing £2,000 raised from his challenge to Sid Williams, founder of a homeless charity in Manchester which provides shelter for rough sleepers in a luxury bus.

A young property mogul has literally answered the prayers of a charity sheltering Manchester's homeless by handing it £2,000 he had left over from a challenge to make himself financially free again.

Sid Williams, founder of Embassy, said he was stunned because he had been praying for help when property entrepreneur Samuel Leeds rang to say he was on his way with a donation.

Not only that, it was the exact amount the charity needed to repair its converted band tour bus after it broke down and blocked junction 1 of the M60. The vehicle provides emergency beds for the city's rough sleepers every day of the year.

"I reckoned it would cost £2,000 to repair it, but knew we didn't have the money, so I started praying for help. Then the next thing I get a call out of the blue from Samuel saying he was heading my way with a cheque for that amount. I just couldn't believe it," said Sid.

"In the end the garage offered to do the repairs for free, so this cash will now pay for 95 nights' off the street for the homeless which is amazing. Over 400 people died through sleeping out in the cold in the UK last year, so this donation may save some lives."

Samuel is the multi-millionaire chairman of Property Investors UK, which teaches thousands of people each year how to achieve financial independence through buying and renting out houses.

The 27-year-old is also a committed Christian who became a property millionaire at the age of just 21 and now owns 30 houses, including a historic country mansion.

More than 10,000 people on his social media challenged him to prove he could build up his portfolio again from scratch.

Samuel responded by going undercover using the pseudonym of Lucas Ruby and setting off with just £50 in his pocket for essentials. He stayed in a hotel in Sheffield, which had been pre-booked for him, and drove around in an old banger. He also wore a disguise because he is so well known in the property world.

In just a week he raised £8,000 from selling various property deals he had sourced to investors. He then put the money into rental apartments to earn a passive monthly income of around £2,000, achieving his aim of becoming financially free again.

As a Christian, his philosophy is not just to encourage people to make as much money as they can, but also to ensure others benefit from their success. He practices what he preaches, with his Midlands-based business raising thousands of pounds each year for charities at home and overseas. One of his proudest achievements was to supply fresh water to a remote Ugandan village where children were suffering badly after having to drink from a lake.

Samuel, who met Sid through The Lions, a Christian organisation for pioneers and entrepreneurs, said: "As part of the challenge I faced being evicted from my hotel if I didn't raise enough money through property deals, and could have been on the street for a while myself. That made me think about Embassy. It's a great feeling to be able to support the excellent work it does for the homeless in Manchester."

The luxury bus, formerly used to ferry top groups, such as Coldplay, to venues, now provides beds for 14 people a night. It is staffed with a permanent manager and a team of volunteers.

Situated in Salford at night, the bus provides homeless people with food, drink and a comfy bed. It also has washing and cooking facilities plus a lounge. People are welcome to remain on the bus until suitable alternative accommodation has been found. Staff work with drug and addiction agencies to ensure clients get the support they need.

The charity is hoping to buy more buses to reduce the number of rough sleepers on Manchester's streets if it can attract enough corporate sponsorship.

"If 30 companies could offer us ongoing sponsorship, it would make an incredible difference to us – even if it is just a couple of thousand pounds a year," said Sid.

The charity is underpinned by a Christian ethos and has been backed by Mayor of Greater Manchester Andy Burnham.

The Embassy bus is featured in a documentary about Samuel Leeds' Financial Freedom Challenge which can be viewed on his YouTube channel. After just two weeks it had already attracted half a million views.

For more information on the Embassy charity visit embassybus.org

Good Samaritan gets an early Christmas present after rescuing a multi-millionaire in disguise

Samuel Leeds pictured with mechanic Tony Tasker after he called in to reward the Good Samaritan with an early Christmas present.

<u>A mechanic, who acted as a Good Samaritan when an old banger broke down on a Sheffield road, was stunned when the driver returned days later with a Christmas present – and revealed he was a multi-millionaire in disguise.</u>

Tony Tasker, who works at Rutland Autos of Sheffield, came to the rescue when he received a phone call from a distressed motorist called 'Lucas Ruby' whose vehicle was stranded near the city centre.

Tony discovered a faulty petrol gauge was to blame as it indicated a good amount of fuel was left in the tank, when in fact it was empty. He then drove Mr Ruby to a petrol station and got him safely back on the road.

When asked how much he was charging for the call-out, the kindly garage worker refused any money and wished the driver a happy Christmas.

Tony later had a surprise visit from the man who handed him a new Samsung mobile phone and a cinema card. Lucas Ruby was in fact Samuel Leeds, a self-made multi-millionaire property investor from the Midlands. He had been on an undercover mission when the 15-year-old car gave up on him. He was wearing a black wig and false glasses.

In real life Samuel Leeds is a committed Christian who runs Property Investors UK, a national training business based at Hilton Hall in Essington, near Wolverhampton. The 27-year-old has taught thousands of people throughout the UK how to achieve financial independence through buying and renting out houses. He owns around 30 houses and was recently featured on TV and in the national press when he acquired Grade II listed Ribbesford House in Worcestershire, one of Britain's most historic country homes.

His philosophy has been to encourage people to make as much money as they can, so long as they look to benefit others too. He practices what he preaches, with his company raising thousands of pounds each year for charities at home and overseas. One of his most rewarding achievements has been to supply fresh water to a remote Ugandan village where children were suffering badly after having to drink from a lake.

The young entrepreneur has always insisted that anyone with the right knowledge can become financially free through property investing – even if they are strapped for cash. Samuel left school at 16 and could have retired by the age of 21 as a result of making a string of shrewd property investments. Recently 10,000 people on social media challenged him to prove he could do it all again from scratch in a different town, and Sheffield was drawn out of a hat.

He was sent to a hotel which had been booked for a week, but with no money to spend, an empty bank account and a zero credit rating. The results of Samuel Leeds's Financial Freedom Challenge will be revealed in a documentary available for viewing on YouTube from Boxing Day.

Speaking of the kindness he received in Sheffield, Samuel said:

"Tony came out and fixed my car during a key moment in the challenge. He could see I was driving a very cheap car and must have thought Lucas Ruby was really struggling for money. When I asked him how much I owed he just said, forget it mate. He was a true Samaritan and the truth was I hardly had anything to give him at that moment anyway.

"I later called the garage and told them who I really was and said I'd like to do something for their mechanic. I asked for any suggestions about what I could buy him. They said he had just smashed his Samsung mobile phone and was a bit upset with the expense of Christmas coming up."

Tony was delighted with his early festive gift, adding: "He seemed like a really nice ordinary guy, who hadn't got a lot to spend on a car. I was shocked when I found out who he really was. I googled his name and it was quite a surprise. I dropped my phone the day before, so it was great to have a new model in time for Christmas."

Claim your FREE Tickets to the
Property Investors Crash Course
now available at:

www.property-investors.co.uk

What are others saying?

Florin Bolojan

"I moved from Romania with nothing and could not speak English. A few years later I have attended the Property Investors Crash Course, done six property deals and now my business is turning over £250,000 per year. I sometimes have to pinch myself because it is although I am dreaming. Samuel even took me to dinner with Robert Kiyosaki to celebrate."

Declan Archer

"After finishing the Royal Marines my dad passed away and I got myself in a financial mess. I wanted to get into property to help support my mum so attended the Property Investors Crash Course. 12 months later I am financially free with a property portfolio that makes a profit of £40,000 per year and am in a position to spend time with my mum and help her financially."

Leah Miller

"My mum and I came to the Property Investors Crash Course with zero property knowledge or experience. Within a matter of weeks we had secured our first Rent-to-Rent which was almost a no-money down deal. We are now making over £100,000 per year through property income, I have quit my job and we are just totally loving life."

Paul and Ann Waters

"Two years ago we had no property investments and were working long hours trading our time for money on a flooring business. Today, we have done over fifty property deals and have made the newspapers for our outstanding property entrepreneurship. It is all down to Samuel's training and the Property Investors Crash Course, we just wish we had started sooner."

Ian Pattison

"I made a decision that I couldn't work in the corporate world forever and needed to create some passive income. After attending the Property Investors Crash Course in Jan 2017 I went on to secure 24 properties within just 18 months. Most of these were Lease Options so I did not need much capital. I have now quit my corporate job and am full time in property. Samuel was just a mentor but is now a friend."

Your Next Steps?

To find out more about the Property Investors Crash Course, please visit:
www.property-investors.co.uk

Alternatively, email info@samuelleeds.com or call 0330 010 0742

Printed in Great Britain
by Amazon

74477351R00059